A SURVIVOR'S GUIDE TO

FAMILIES

WAYLAND

First published in 1999 by Wayland Publishers Limited

61 Western Road, Hove, East Sussex BN3 1JD

© Copyright 1999 Wayland Publishers Limited

Illustrations © Polly Dunbar 1999

Editor: Liz Gogerly

British Library Cataloguing in Publication Data

Baker, Jeanette

Survivor's guide to families

1. Family – Juvenile literature 2. Teenagers – Life skill guides

I. Title II. Dunbar, Polly III. Families

302.3'4'0835

ISBN 07502 2621 8

ISBN 07502 2475 4

Design and typesetting: Leist

Printed and bound in Great E

About the author...

Jeanette has worked for several teenage magazines including *Just Seventeen, LOOKS, more!* and finally *MIZZ,* where she was editor. She now lives in London with her husband and their cat, Bunny. As the youngest of three children she spent all her family car journeys squashed in the middle, but other than that generally got away with murder. She'd like to take this opportunity to thank her mum and dad, and her brother and sister, for putting up with those oh so interesting tantrums she had as a teenager. She'd also like to thank Andrew Dean and members of Finchley Youth Theatre and the pupils of Lewes Priory for helping her with this book.

About the illustrator...

Polly used to live on a hill in Norwich with her parents, her older brother Ben, a cat and mice. She now lives on the seafront in Brighton with her mates and a family of sea monkeys. She has been drawing cartoons since she was fourteen and goes to Brighton Art School.

Also available in the series:

FRIENDS   LOVE ETC
SCHOOL

contents...

Happy
families?

It all starts here...

You've just picked up a book about coping with families, which probably means that yours are driving you insane at the moment. So first of all, good work! By reaching for this book, you're doing something constructive about the situation rather than slamming your bedroom door for the five-hundredth time or packing up your belongings in a spotted handkerchief à la Dick Whittington. So why are they driving you mad? Many of the problems you'll face as you hit adolescence will stem from the fact that it's a struggle to make your families aware that you are not, in fact, eight years old any more:

'Mum, dad, face it – the days of My Little Pony and Thomas the Tank Engine are over. I can make it all the way to the bus stop without an armed escort, and yes I did eat some breakfast.'

'Come on, one spoonful for me and one for the ponies.'

If only it was that simple

And what happens when you try to make them see reason? You get hit with the 'But we're only doing/saying this because we care about you' cliché, which is all very well, but it doesn't stop them from making your life a misery does it? That's where this Survivor's Guide comes in. Families are tricky and occasionally complex customers and you'll need all the advice you can get to negotiate your way through your teenage years with minimum aggro. You never know, you may even end up liking each other!

Aargh

Exactly what planet are you from dad?

I f only your family was normal – wouldn't life be so much easier? Your mates' families seem normal enough – they don't behave strangely, wear odd clothes, say ridiculous things or misunderstand every word you utter, so why are the members of your family such a disaster?

Tell me about it

'When I go out with my parents they can be very embarrassing. When we go to restaurants my mum always complains about things really loudly, and everyone looks at us.' **Sandra, 13**

'My family are always so loud – I wish I had a t-shirt I could wear that says "I don't belong to them".' **Nick, 14**

'If we're going out to a party or a barbeque, my mum always says, "Luke you must bring your guitar so that we can all have a sing around the campfire". She has no concept of how humiliating that is.' **Luke, 13**

'My parents are so embarrassing at Parents' Evenings – they just wander around smiling at complete strangers and saying things like, "Hello, what's your name then?" What a nightmare.' **Alan, 12**

hello

'Look what I've found dear. Shall we treat it as our own?'

So why are your family so odd?

There are two possible explanations:

1 You were kidnapped at birth by aliens disguising themselves as unfashionable human beings who wanted to learn about planet earth whilst at the same time causing you untold grief and embarrassment.

2 If you asked your mates about their apparently 'normal' families, they'd be able to list just as many grievances about theirs as you can about yours. Which roughly translates as:

THERE IS NO SUCH THING AS NORMAL!!!

Still not convinced? OK, fingers on buzzers...

(a)

Q: What is a normal family?

A: Simple – it's a mum, a dad, two kids (one boy, one girl) and a really cute dog/cat/bunny/goldfish (please delete as applicable) who all live in a house that looks like (a). This may be the case in schmaltzy Hollywood films, or cheesy children's books, but you only have to look around at the other kids in your class at school, or the families who live in your street to see that there really isn't such a thing as 'a normal family'.

Yeah, right!

Way back in the dark ages when your parents were growing up, the 'average' family may well have consisted of a mum, dad and a couple of kids, but this simply isn't the case any more. A family can consist of all sorts of combinations of people – none of them necessarily better or worse than the other...

Parents, one or two?

Some people call them 'single parents'; others refer to them as 'lone parents'. You probably just call them 'mum' or 'dad', which is altogether more sensible. If you live with just one parent, it doesn't mean you'll have more or fewer problems than people who live with two – just different ones. Ask a friend who lives with their mum and dad and they may envy you for only having to deal with one of the set. You, on the other hand, might feel short changed for not having the full monty. Neither situation is right or wrong, and it's really up to you and your mum, or dad, to make it work as well as possible.

Taking one 'step' at a time

'Yes, that's Andrew's mum and dad – but it's not his 'real dad'. Er, excuse me, what's a 'real dad'? And is an 'unreal dad' one that's made out of empty washing-up bottles and sticky-backed plastic? Probably not. When people talk about someone not being a 'real' or 'proper' mum, dad, brother or sister, they're probably referring to stepfamily members.

So how does a person like you end up with a stepfamily then? Well believe it or not, adults over the age of thirty are still capable of falling in love – scary but true. So if your mum and dad are no longer together it's feasible that either or both of them may fall in love with someone else. It's then perfectly natural for them to want to commit to that other person by either moving in or getting married. Which is why there are plenty of families around including step- mums, dads, brothers and sisters.

N.B. Contrary to most childhood fairy stories, not all step-people are evil, they very rarely lock you in rat-infested cellars and only very occasionally do they stop you from going to the ball.

'Hang on a minute, you're not a real dad.'

And on the subject of 'real' parents...

It's one of life's little mysteries. Those who live with adoptive or foster parents may, on occasion, wish they could find and/or live with their birth or natural parents, while those who live with their birth parents may sometimes find themselves wondering if that nice couple down the road would adopt them so they can 'GET-THE-HELL-OUT-OF-THIS-HOUSE!!'. Whatever way you look at it, whether you're adopted or fostered it certainly shouldn't affect how much you are loved by your family.

unreal

My two dads (or mums)

Having two dads, or two mums, i.e gay parents, might not be a situation you come across every day, but many single-sex couples may have children from previous heterosexual relationships, or through adoption. Unfortunately, because some people, adults and kids alike, are very narrow-minded, uninformed or just plain stupid, they may try to tell you that gay parents are 'wrong' or 'not natural'. However being gay doesn't automatically stop a person, male or female, from wanting children, or from being an excellent and loving parent.

House dads & working mums!

- 'A woman's place is in the home – cooking, sewing, cleaning and bringing up kids'.
- 'A man's place is out at work, earning a crust, bringing home the bacon and working his way up the career ladder'.

Now, back in the real world...

It may have been the case way back in your grandparents' days that it was very rare for a woman to go out to work once she'd had children, and almost unheard of for dads to be the ones who stayed at home in order to bring up the kids. These days both situations are becoming more and more common. There could be any number of reasons for this, e.g. if both your parents work, it may be because they need two salaries in order to keep you in Playstations and Nike trainers. Alternatively, your mum may feel she wants to keep working in order to keep her brain ticking over and her place on the career ladder. Either way, it may mean your mum and dad aren't always there exactly when you want them to be, but it can also mean you get some precious space and free time around the house. It doesn't mean that they think their work is more important than their children, or that they can't really be bothered with that 'bringing up kids thing'.

families - who needs them?

Although most of the time your family seem to get on your nerves, please remember that every now and then they can come in useful. The next time you want to kill the lot of them (see the 'Can't live with 'em' list), try to remember that they do have their uses (see the 'Can't live without 'em' list).

Can't live with 'em

• They know exactly how to wind you up, and do – often.

• Their favourite pastime is embarrassing you in front of your friends.

• They're always hanging around when you don't want them to.

• They love saying 'No' or 'You can't' whenever you want something.

• They don't listen properly to half the things you say.

Tell me about it

'Sometimes I dress pretty scruffily, but my mum always tries to smarten me up and make me look girlie in a skirt and blouse and stuff.' **Nicola, 11**

'Sometimes parents just don't get it. My mum will say, "It's raining, you'd better put a mac on," and she can't understand why I don't want to go to school in a mac! She'll say pointless things like, "But everyone wears macs, what's your problem?" Is she serious?' **Martin, 14**

'When my parents' friends come round to visit, my dad always makes me play my flute and then they'll all clap at the end. It makes me feel about five years old.' **Richard, 13**

'Play nicely or the cat gets it.'

If you just had to cope with your family constantly getting on your nerves then life wouldn't be so bad, but as well as the irritation factor you also have to deal with them constantly sticking their noses into your business. Ever feel as though families don't understand the concept of 'privacy' or 'This is my life so please just butt out!'?

oh please!

'Well I never there's my Radio Times.'

Tell me about it

'If any girls from school call me at home, I have to go to the bottom of the garden to talk to them or face total humiliation from my family.' **Daniel, 14**

'When I'm on the phone my mum will walk into the living room and pretend to look around for the Radio Times, but I know she's only hanging around to try and listen in to the conversation.' **Natalie, 12**

'My parents don't understand me. They think they understand – but they don't. Money, friends, school – they don't get any of it, and it really frustrates me that when we argue they've got an answer for everything. They'll say something clever and all I can say in return is "Yes, but, er um...". Then I just leg it to my bedroom and think of what I should have said.'
Louise, 14

can't live without 'em

- They know exactly how to cheer you up, and do – when you let them!
- They know you inside out, and you can totally be yourself around them.
- They're always there for you when you really need them.
- They come in handy when you want some money/new clothes/to borrow a CD/to eat.
- When they do actually sit down and listen to you, they usually dish out some pretty useful advice if you have a problem.

'There you go, that put a smile on your face.'

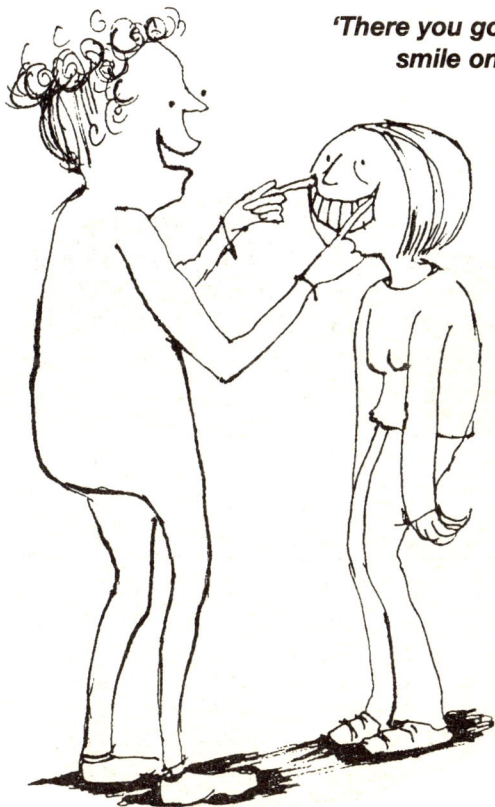

If anyone asked you if your family are good in a crisis, you'd probably laugh in their face and tell them to get real. But if you really think about it, when you do actually sit down and talk to your family they can turn out to be quite useful.

oh yeah

Tell me about it

'Parents can be useful when you need money... and lifts.' **Lorna, 14**

'You hate to admit it but sometimes parents can give out some pretty good advice. I suppose it's because they've been around longer and they have experienced stuff that we haven't.' **Billy, 12**

'Older brothers and sisters can be useful at school if there's something horrible going on. They can also usually give good advice because they're older, but not as old and out of it as your parents.'
Lucy, 11

'If someone's very ill or has died then you probably want to talk to your family about it rather than your friends.' **Niall, 12**

'Sometimes you can trust your family more than your friends. If you tell your friend about a problem they might spread it, but you know your mum won't tell anyone.'
Susan, 13

'So sis, where are we off to tonight?'

'It's quite good having an older sister, especially if she's been pretty sensible because then your parents go easier on you and usually let you do more, younger.' **Melissa, 12**

'I suppose if you haven't got anything to do and your mates aren't around then you can always do something with your family.' **Will, 14**

'My dad can be quite a laugh sometimes - when it's just me and him we usually have a really good time.' **Ian, 14**

families – a user's guide...

Want to survive your teenage years and still have a family who will talk to you at the end of them? Yes? Then there are two ways of playing this...

1 You stay in your room for the next eight years avoiding any contact with them whatsoever, in order to prevent hostility or conflict. This is an interesting option, however, it's not one that you are advised to take as: a) it's next to impossible to carry out (they'll find a way into your bedroom and start telling you to tidy it up before you've had the chance to evict them), and b) it's very dull.

2 You use a cunning and insightful 'user's guide' (remarkably like this one) to work out what makes the various members of your family tick, and how to use this information to your own advantage.

If you have opted for option two, please turn to page 24 now. If you have opted for option one, you'd best get up to your room now with this and many, many other books...

How to handle your mum

The problems...

The 'mother' member of the family is possibly the most complex and one of the most important to crack if you are to glide effortlessly through your teenage years, but it's not always easy. Any of the following sound familiar?

Tell me about it

'When I need some new shoes or trainers my mum just doesn't understand why I need the ones I want. She'll just say, "What's the big deal about having a tick on the back?"!' **Jason, 13**

'When I'm on the phone to a girl, my mum always sings really loudly in the background. It will usually be mushy songs which makes it even worse.' **David, 12**

'Usually my mum is quite good at dressing, but sometimes she will wear the most embarrassing clothes – with bows! I try to tell her, but she won't listen.'
Lucy, 11

'My mum says she likes a lot of the music I like, but sometimes I wish she didn't – especially when she tries to sing along to the records on the radio.' **Claire, 12**

'My mum always tells me to do up my shoes properly – even when it's my trainers – and she does it in front of my friends! Recently she used black shoe polish to colour in the white bits of my trainers because school uniform is supposed to be black shoes only. She tried to say that they looked OK, but I'm the one who has to wear them to school, not her.' **Lee, 14**

mothers!

'Mum, mum! Easy on the bows...'

How to spot a mum...

What she'll say:

Her favourite phrases are 'No', 'You've got to be joking', 'Don't talk to me like that young lady/young man' and, 'I said NO!'.

(a)

What she'll wear:

It will either be something incredibly unfashionable and distinctly lacking in style (see a), or worse still, something trendy that should only be worn by someone half her age (see b). Either way she can't win because let's face it, she's a mum, and the fashion police have been on surveillance duty here for some time.

(b)

What she'll do:

• Make your life a misery whenever possible.

• Constantly remind you that your friends are better behaved/more sensibly dressed/less lippy than you are.

• Invent new rules as and when she feels like it, and justify each of these with the all-encompassing phrase, 'Because I say so'.

- Sing – usually very badly, loudly, out of tune and always while you're on the phone to your mates or in some other equally embarrassing situation.

When she'll come in useful:

- Handing out money (but not as frequently as you'd like).
- Providing food and a roof over your head (often a joint effort with dad figure).
- Supplying clothing (usually too cheap, the wrong type, the wrong size and never enough).

'Because I say so...'

How to handle her...

I t's going to be tough, but try to avoid getting into confrontational situations with your mum – they'll only escalate and nine times out of ten, she'll be the one who walks away the victor, and you'll be... back in your room! Instead, try the more mature approach. On occasions when you'd usually start the sentence with, 'You're talking complete rubbish, you mad woman', try replacing this with the more diplomatic, 'I can see your point of view mum, however...'. Once she's recovered from the shock of you not storming off in a huff, she may actually listen to the end of the sentence and take your point into consideration.

Top Tip

Another tip is to cleverly adapt the, 'But Michael's mum lets him (fill in the blank) so why can't I?' tactic. Instead of always rattling on about how cool/flexible/ understanding your mates' parents are, try a bit of flattery on yours instead, e.g. 'I've just spoken to my friend Rebecca. She's just had another huge row with her mum. I'm so glad we get on as well as we do, aren't you mum? By the way, is it still OK for me to get those Calvin Klein jeans I saw on Saturday?'. Yeah, yeah, it may be a long shot, but it's worth a try isn't it?

How to handle your dad

The problems...

Dads, like mums, can be pretty tricky customers. Most of the time they appear distant and disinterested in your life and then just when you want them to turn a blind eye, they come down on you like a ton of bricks. Don't ever underestimate the input of a dad on a family matter or you could land yourself in trouble.

Tell me about it

'When I have sleep-overs with my friends, my dad will come downstairs wearing his really embarrassing pyjamas and say, "Keep it down will you girls? And isn't it time you were asleep by now?" How embarrassing is that?!'
Lisa, 11

'My dad thinks he's quite hip when it comes to music, so if I go to a concert he'll insist on coming with me. Then he'll start dancing when no one else is – and he's a really embarrassing dancer.' **Lyndsey, 12**

'Dad, I think you should just SHUT UP!'

'I've been saying,'Shut up' all my life and now my dad has suddenly decided that he doesn't like it so I have to stop! If he'd told me this when I was three years old then I could probably cope with it, but why has he suddenly decided to move the goal posts?' **Vanessa, 13**

annoying

How to spot a dad...

What he'll say:

He may look like he would need that newspaper surgically removed from his nose before he joined in the 'lively debate' about you staying out until eleven on Friday nights, but the second you count on his support – bam! He's in there with a moving story about how, 'in his day' you had to be home by four in the afternoon and ready for bed by five, like it or not. Sad... but true.

Other favourite dad phrases include...'Ask your mother', 'Not if I have anything to do with it', and the classic, 'If you think you're going out looking like that, you've got another think coming.' Obviously some of these phrases are interchangeable with 'mum speak' and vice versa.

What he'll wear:

If he thinks he's cool, jeans with a crease up the front where they've been ironed. You will also find a wardrobe stuffed with 'unusual' jumpers, dull work clothes and a selection of grotty tracksuits which he insists on wearing out on trips to DIY stores.

What he'll do:

• Grunt agreement with your mum when he hasn't even listened to the conversation/ argument.

Do-it-yourself hell

• Insist that you recount every single question from last week's geography test, along with all of your answers – as if the experience in itself wasn't painful enough the first time around.

• Scratch himself in embarrassing places when your mates are there.

• Tell you to turn that pop music down and go and tidy your room - even though he hasn't been in your room for three months.

not cool

When he'll come in useful:

• As a taxi service (if you can bear the humiliation of him shouting, 'I'm over here Pumpkin!' across the road).

• Handing out money (as long as he hasn't conferred with your mum previously).

• Providing all that roof-over-your-head-food-on-your-plate-you-don't-know-how-lucky-you-are parent stuff that gets trotted out when you are 'being ungrateful again!'.

How to handle him...

Keep it simple. As far as a dad is concerned, the quicker any 'family situation' can be sorted out, the better, so don't just present him with a problem – give him a solution as well.
E.g. 'Dad, we have a problem with the phone – mum says she needs to use it, but I'm waiting for a really important call from Andrew about tomorrow's French test. Now if I had a separate line and a phone in my room, we wouldn't have this dilemma would we?'. You never know... it might work!

How to handle your older sister/brother

The problems...

Beware the older sibling – he/she has more experience of parent handling and may have height/weight advantages over you too...

Tell me about it

'My older sister is always whingeing about how when she was my age she wasn't allowed to do this, that or the other, or that she had to go to bed at 7.30 – which is so not true.' **Michael, 11**

'When my older sister decides she doesn't like something in her wardrobe, she tells my mum that it's too small for her, then I'm made to have it and she gets something new! How unfair is that?!' **Anna, 12**

nightmare

'My older sister is so embarrassing in school – she'll come up to me in front of my friends and say, "Hi honey how are you?" in a sickly voice. Then she'll start hugging and kissing me. And her friends will say, "Oh your little sister's so sweet!". I wouldn't mind but they're only two years older than me!' **Michelle, 12**

'My older brother always borrows my things without asking and then when I ask to borrow something of his he always says no! And I always end up clearing up after him.' **Tom, 11**

'Ahh, your little sister is so cute.'

How to spot an older sister or brother...

What they'll say:

'Go away' is always popular along with 'I'll kill you', 'Shut UP', and 'Get out of my room'. These straightforward and easily comprehensible instructions should be followed to the letter if physical violence is to be avoided. You can also spot an older sibling by the common use of the 'It's not fair, I wasn't allowed to do that when I was his/her age' declaration. This is a direct tactic designed to make your life a misery by pointing out to parents the irregularities of their child-rearing tactics, and even though it rarely works, they'll keep on using it in the hope that one day your parents see the error of their ways...

Dream on, big sister/brother!

go away!

'Hey mum, the brat's annoying me again.'

What they'll wear:

All the clothes you're not allowed to... except in two years time when they're totally unfashionable, threadbare and have an interesting collection of stains all over them – that's when they get 'handed down' to you. Whoopee!

What they'll do:

- Stomp about a lot, slamming doors – take note of their technique, you could probably learn something.
- Moan (usually at you/about you/to you).
- Employ physical violence against you whenever your parents aren't looking.
- Taunt you with the amount of pocket money they receive/the clothes they're allowed to wear/how late they're allowed to stay out.

When they'll come in useful:

Whereas your older siblings think you're 'whiny, annoying and stupid', their friends often think you're 'cute, funny and adorable'. When these friends also happen to be attractive, popular and go to the same school as you, they can come in extremely handy!

• When you want to moan to someone about parent problems, they'll understand more than anybody else where you're coming from because they've probably been through the same thing already.

• Discussing 'delicate' and 'personal' problems or concerns. As long as you can trust them not to blab to the entire school, an older brother or sister will often be easier and less embarrassing to talk to than a parent about relationships/sex/body matters or school worries.

• Borrowing their things. After all they've got loads more stuff than you, so surely they won't miss the odd CD here and there.

How to handle them...

As mentioned earlier, knowing when to keep to the 'Go away' instruction is always a good starting point in dealing with older brothers and sisters, as the less you irritate them, the more useful they will be to you in the long run. Try to avoid running to your mum or dad to complain every time an older sibling annoys you as this will really get their back up. And if you want to survive long enough to see your 18th birthday, never, ever stand behind your parents grinning as they scream, 'You're old enough to know better' at your older brother or sister.

How to handle
your younger
sister/brother

The problems...

Everything was fine until they came along. You were just getting the hang of this parent/child relationship thing when out pops 'Junior' and screws everything up. Great!

Little brothers and sisters... aren't they sweet – NOT! The thing is, although they tend to be smaller and weedier, the option to pummel them until they shut up is not a good one. You can guarantee that no matter how weak they claim you've left them, they'll always have enough strength left to crawl to your mum and dad, and enough breath left in them to splutter... 'It was your other child who did this to me!!'.

'Look mum he's pulled both my hands off.'

Tell me about it

'I had to wait ages before my mum and dad would let me go out on my own, but now my little sister is being allowed to do the same things at a much younger age. It drives me mad.' **Simone, 13**

'My sister will go on and on until you kick her, then when she's sure there's something to see she rushes off screaming to my mum to show her.' **Philippa, 14**

'My little brother used to be so sweet – he'd play with his train set and talk and sing to himself, but now he practises his karate on me and never wants to watch the same things on the TV.' **Clare, 14**

'My little sister is always going in my room to play, even though she knows she's not allowed in there. I wouldn't mind, but she leaves all her dollies and all her little toys in there when I'm not looking, then my friends come round and see them!'
Tim, 14

The only thing for it is to bite your lip when they're stressing you out, and instead of ignoring them, shouting at them or hitting them, get them on your side – believe it or not they can come in useful for all sorts of things.

How to spot a younger sister/brother...

What they'll say:

Whenever anything goes horribly wrong in the house, the phrase, 'It wasn't my fault', is usually trotted out by younger siblings. This will be accompanied by a wide-eyed, innocent glance in your direction resulting in your parents blaming and punishing you... for everything. Other favourite sayings include, 'I'll tell mum', 'But I want to come too', and 'I hate you', all said in a whiny, high-pitched voice designed to irritate.

What they'll wear:

Whatever they flippin' well like because, let's face it, they get everything they want whenever they want it. When it comes to clothing your adorable baby brother or sister, it would appear that your parents have forgotten those silly old rules about wearing something until it doesn't fit anymore – because they seem to be getting new clothes all the time!

'Oy! Mum said to take turns.'

What they'll do:

Whine, moan, get on your nerves, follow you about, go in your room when you've told them not to, borrow things without asking and then never give them back (or if they do, only when they're broken/ruined).

When they'll come in useful:

• For fetching and carrying your things, e.g. drinks, snacks, your shoes, magazines. Basically, if you've got them trained correctly you can send them off hunting for anything that isn't within easy reach.

• Being used as decoys to distract your parents. If you want to get everyone off your case, send in Junior to entertain and keep everyone occupied while you go about your business.

• Someone to have a laugh with when your mates aren't around. Yes, believe it or not, if you make the effort to devote some time to the little sprog, you may discover that he/she actually possesses something resembling a sense of humour.

How to handle them...

It's all about patience. If you can take a deep breath and count to ten silently while they're winding you up, you can then take the more mature approach to this older/younger sibling arrangement. Make the most of the fact that somewhere deep inside them, they probably look up to you and in many ways admire you. Use this admiration sensibly and you may find yourself with a helpful little ally.

favourite family bust-ups

Ever feel like you seem to spend most of your time at home arguing with your parents? That's probably because you do! But don't give up on them just yet, and don't stress yourself out thinking that it's just your family who are particularly hopeless. We asked approximately ten billion families what the most common causes of family rows tended to be and they all said the following...

The top five favourite family arguments...

1 **Money** – Parents think you want too much. You think they never supply enough.

2 **Clothes** – They think whatever you wear is either too scruffy/too grown up/too short/too tight, and always too expensive. You think they should leave the fashion advice to people who don't spend their lives in nylon and polyester.

3 **Going out** – They think you go out too much, you stay out too late, and you hang around with the wrong people. You think they should get out of the house more.

4 **House Rules** – They think you should pull your weight more around the house. You think they should have considered hiring servants rather than having children.

5 **School** – They think you don't take it seriously enough. You think they should spend a day at your school and then they'd realize that you have to have a sense of humour to stay there or you'd go mad.

unfair

'Dad, I'm pleased to see you taking school so seriously.'

other popular themes for 'discussion' can include:

● How unfair it is that your brother/sister seems to get away with so much more than you.

● Bad manners, bad language, bad attitude – according to your parents you adopt all three far too regularly.

● You're growing up too quickly and you'll have to wait until you're older before you can do 98 per cent of the things you want to.

● Phone and TV wars. They're only domestic appliances, but they can be the root of many a family argument. Ask your parents and they'll say you spend far too long on the phone and you only ever watch rubbish on the telly. And their problem is...?

Some of these situations may sound familiar, and even if they don't you could probably replace them with about 65 of your own. But believe it or not, there are ways of dealing with 'disagreements' like these so that you don't have to go over them again... and again... and again.

Tell me about it

'My dad has got this thing about bad manners, and he's constantly on my case about it, which totally stresses me out. If I ever swear by accident, he'll say, "I bet your friend Naomi doesn't swear".' **Gemma, 13**

'I don't understand why my mum gets so annoyed when I leave my room in a tip – it's my room, she doesn't have to go in there!' **Ben, 13**

'I seem to be rowing with my mum and dad about home-work a lot these days. Even if I haven't got any, they expect me to be doing some! They don't believe me when I say I've done it. What do they want me to do – make it up?' **Adam, 14**

'I've been begging my mum to buy me some Levis, but she just says, "What's wrong with the jeans you've already got?" Duh! They're not Levis mum! They're horrible.' **Sam, 13**

'When I ask my mum if I can go out she'll say, "Yes but only when you've finished your homework, cleared up your bedroom, got your school bag ready for tomorrow and washed your hair" Well who's got time to go out after they've done all that?' **Theresa, 13**

'When I watch Neighbours it drives my parents mad. They think it's complete rubbish and will say "Why are you wasting your time watching this stuff?".' **Jo, 14**

How to live with your family... without going completely insane

You may spend your days dreaming of a time when you can return home to your own flat or house after a hard day at work or college. You may even smile to yourself as you imagine throwing your coat on the floor, emptying the contents of your bag out onto the sofa and turning the music up extremely loud (even though the telly's on) before digging into an evening meal consisting of chips from the chip shop, a Mars Bar and very definitely no vegetables. However, back in the real world, you still have several years of 'living at home' to get through first, and there are ways and means of surviving this process...

There's no place like (leaving) home.

Living with the system

Some of them may seem ridiculous, some of them will drive you mad, but the fact of the matter is, there will always be rules and regulations that everyone has to stick to if you and your family are going to live in the same house without killing each other. Obviously these will vary from home to home depending on how strict or relaxed your parents are, but before you even think about whingeing to your mum and dad that your mates don't have to put up with the same things you do, save your breath. This will only serve to wind parents up, and will probably result in them concocting even more ridiculous regulations for you to keep to. There are better ways to cope with disagreements and upheavals at home...

Question:

How am I supposed to avoid getting in trouble when my family keep making up the rules about staying out late/bringing friends home/watching videos/playing on the computer/homework as they go along?

Answer:

Some of the worst rows within families often happen through misunderstandings, so if necessary call a house meeting where everyone can discuss the rules. Once they're set, however, it's then up to you to stick to them if you don't want trouble!

'Ooh, I get it, you're only allowed out until 3am every other night.'

Question:

I'm always the one who ends up doing the washing up and clearing away in our house, while my younger brother and sister do nothing. When I complain to my mum and step dad about it, it ends up in a row. What should I do?

Answer:

If it always seems to be one person who gets lumbered with the grotty jobs in the house – whether that's you, your mum, your dad, or one of your brothers or sisters – sooner or later they're going to lose it. To prevent this, the whole family should agree on a rota so that everyone has to do their fair share of jobs around the house. This way nobody can get fed up about being picked on.

Question:

I've been feeling really depressed lately about the amount of work I've got to do before my exams, and all my family seem to do is moan at me. How can I get them off my case?

Answer:

Before you completely write off your family as useless and un-supportive, ask yourself how often you actually talk to them about what's happening in your life. And do they ever explain their problems or worries to you? It's usually when we're feeling miserable or depressed that we take it out on the people closest to us – and that usually means family. The thing is, it's a lot easier to cope with a person's bad moods if you know why they're behaving like that. So the next time a so-called friend gives you grief, or you're worried about your exams, get it off your chest by telling someone at home. Not only will they understand why you've been moody and miserable, talking about it will probably make you feel better and they may even suggest some solutions to your problems. This works both ways, so you could do worse than ask if there's anything the matter or anything you can do to help the next time a member of your family looks fed-up.

Keeping the peace

f you decide that enough is enough, and you're fed-up with arguing with your family the whole time, there are ways of dealing with the situation that don't involve screaming, door slamming or sulking... honestly.

The Golden Rules of Family Rows...

I Think before you scream

You may have got in the habit with your mum/dad/brother/sister of always expecting the worst, so that whenever they start to bring up a controversial subject, you're there and ready with your defence. Before you know it, voices are raised and you've stomped off to your room with the words, 'You're grounded' ringing in your ears. Next time, try taking a deep breath, then take the time to think about what's been said before responding. When you do reply, don't automatically raise your voice or get angry and upset. Keep in mind that you want to 'sort this out' and the more time you take to respond, the more likely you are to come out with a sensible reply that will have far better results than just another slanging match.

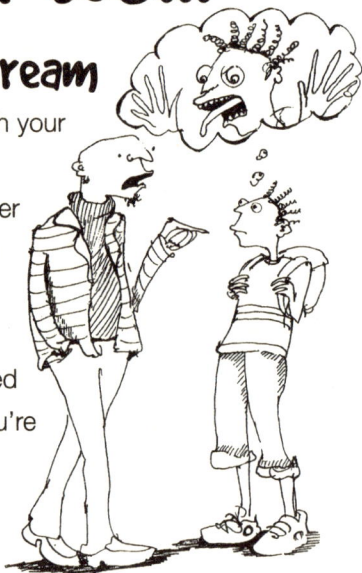

'Guess what mum, I'm pregnant too.'

2 Choose your moment

If you know you've got to talk about something at home that's liable to cause trouble, don't just rush in from school and go for it the second your bag hits the floor. Before you even think about starting this, you need to suss out the following...

• is whoever you want to speak to in a pretty good mood?
• are they busy or distracted doing something else?
• have you got the time and privacy to discuss the matter properly?

By choosing the right moment, even if that means delaying the conversation for an hour or a day, you are far more likely to get the results you're after.

3 Know when to negotiate

The art of winning an argument often means having to surrender certain things along the way, so rather than reaching a stalemate where nobody's happy, work out between you if there are any areas of compromise. Make it clear that you are willing to negotiate if they are. This will show whoever it is you're arguing with that you really do want to work this out sensibly rather than scream and shout until you get your own way.

'Hey, how about you let go of my neck and I'll stop punching you.'

'Oh I see, you didn't really mean it when you called me a green, hairy-legged squid.'

4 Learn to listen

It's amazing how many arguments develop when people don't listen and then get the wrong end of the stick. It's easy to fly off the handle when you think someone has said something totally out of order, when actually they haven't said anything of the sort. Whatever it is that you're having to discuss, ask the member of your family who you're arguing with to listen to you for five minutes without interrupting so that you can explain your point of view. Once you've got your point across give them their five minutes, and really try to listen to what they're saying without getting angry.

Now you know the golden rules, try applying them to some specific situations. Any of these arguments on the next few pages sound vaguely familiar...?

Homework Hell

They say: 'You never spend enough time on your homework.'

You say: 'How do you know how much time I should be spending on my homework, are you psychic?'

Result: You are banished to your room and told not to come out until you've learnt some respect.

The better way: Your parents may think you're not spending enough time on your homework because as far as they can tell you simply disappear into your room each evening after school, turn on your radio and then re-emerge some time later muttering, 'I'm going out'. They may not even realize you've touched your homework – after all, as far as they're concerned it must take you all night to make your room as messy as it is. No wonder they're giving you grief about the lack of homework scenario.

'Dad, I don't think you appreciate how long it takes me to get my room like this...'

Communication is the key here. As soon as you arrive home from school, make the effort to say hello, smile (simple but effective) and then tell your mum or dad what kind of homework you've got, how long you think it will take you and that you're going to your room to get started now. Then, if you finish in roughly the amount of time you specified, everyone will be cool about it. If it doesn't take as long, explain to your parents how pleased you are that it seemed more straightforward than you first thought – they'll probably be impressed that you're coping so well. If it ends up taking longer than you first thought, they'll simply think how diligent and conscientious you are. It's a can't fail scenario.

Result!!

Revision Divisions

They say: 'You'll never pass your exams if you carry on going out this much with your friends. When on earth are you going to revise?'

You say: 'I am revising, all the time, but I have to get out of this house sometimes. And anyway, what's the point in me getting qualifications if, by the time I've got them, I've been driven totally mad by my parents because they've locked me in my room day and night?'

Result: You are banished to your room (again), and told not to come out until you've learnt some respect.

The better way: Explain to your parents that you work better if you have regular breaks and distractions, then ask them to help you devise a revision timetable which incorporates time for chilling out and relaxing with friends. This way both you and your parents will have a clear idea of how much work there is to be done in the build up to the exams and as long as you stick to it, this should prevent them from getting shirty when you do go out.

chill out

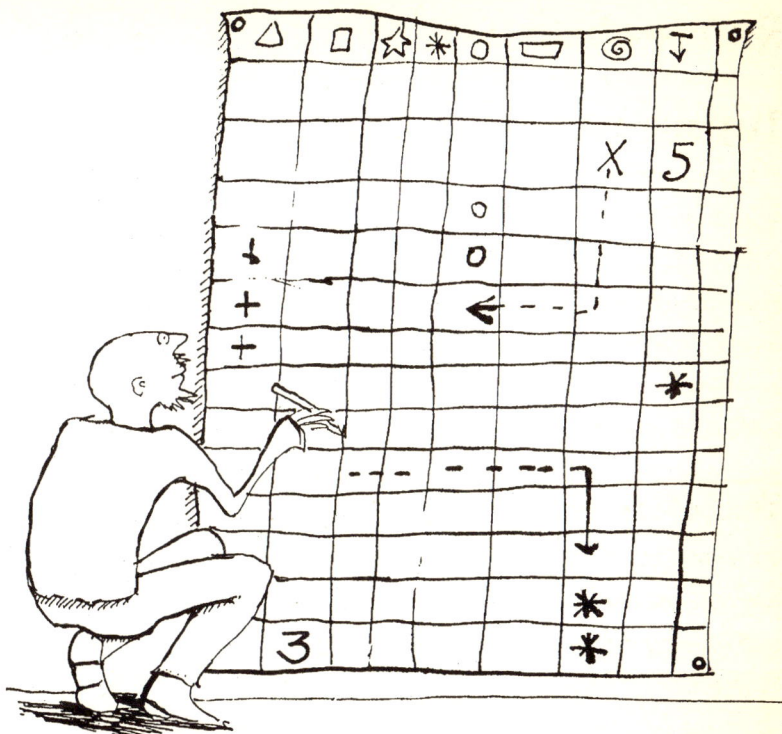

'Thanks dad, you're doing a great job.'

Report riots

They say: 'You'd better have a good explanation for this appalling report young man/lady, or you won't be leaving this house until you're 18.'

You say: 'Actually I have got an explanation – all of my teachers are psychos who hate me. Plus the fact that they wouldn't know a good pupil if one came along and hit them over the head with a baseball bat. So who are you going to believe, them or me?'

Result: You are banished to your room, etc., etc..

'Excuse me sir, I don't think we understand each other.'

The better way: This is a tough one because there's not much arguing with what's down there in black and white. If the report really is that bad, the humble, grovelling, apologetic approach, although painful short-term, is probably the best option. This is one of those rare occasions when you should just take yourself off to your room before you've even been told to, and DON'T slam the door. If, however, your parents are over-reacting somewhat to the odd low-light of an otherwise 'OK' report, still do the apology thing, but point out that it's not all bad news, and promise you'll try harder next term.

'See dad, I love you so much more than school.'

family Vs friends

They say: 'Where did you learn that kind of language? It's from those dreadful people you call friends isn't it? They're a bad influence on you and I'm not happy about you spending time with them.'

You say: 'Erm, excuse me, do I tell you who you should and shouldn't like? And if I did, would you take any notice? I don't think so!'

The results: Your parents pull strange, pinched faces whenever they see you with your mates, while you spend more and more time 'out' because you feel uncomfortable about bringing friends home.

'I'm sorry dad, but I don't think much of your new wife.'

The better way: Unless your friends really are dodgy (in which case why are you hanging around with them?), take the time to remind your parents of that well-worn phrase 'never judge a book by its cover', then suggest that they actually meet and talk to your friends. Once they have spent some time with them, hopefully they will realize that you are not in fact hanging around with potential drug dealers/armed robbers/muggers, and that should make them less uptight.

N.B. Try to encourage your friends not to swear, spit or kick the dog while they are having this nice chat with your parents!

'Mum, meet my mates.'

The 'Why can't you be more like...' factor

They say: 'I bet your friends don't talk to their parents like this. Why can't you be more like that nice Richard? Or Vanessa down the road? She's always so polite and sweet.'

You say: 'Aaaaaaaaaaaargh! I can't flippin' win. One minute my friends are a bad influence on me, the next you want to adopt them and get rid of me! Perhaps Vanessa's so sweet because she hasn't had to live with YOU for the past 13 years!'

The result: Doors slam, everyone screams and your parents start to seriously consider a child-swap arrangement with Vanessa's parents.

The better way: It's a tricky one this, because you may feel that ultimately it's your parents who are responsible for your behaviour, after all, they're the ones who brought you up aren't they? However, suggesting they go and get some 'parenting tips' from Vanessa's parents may not be the most diplomatic thing to do. If you don't want to be having the same argument again next week, try taking the mature approach – think about what it is you did that wound them up and try to avoid doing it again in the future – that way you're taking away their ammunition for next time.

'I'll swap you my whole family for your lovely Vanessa.'

The argument: Bedroom Bust-ups

They say: 'If I have to tell you to tidy up your room one more time, you're grounded... for ever!'

You say: 'It's my room and I like it that way, so get off my case.'

The result: 'You are grounded... for ever.'

The better way: Compromise is the key to this one. If you leave your room looking like a tip, regardless of how much you like it that way, your mum or dad will be on your back about it all the time until you tidy up. In order to give them one less thing to moan about, ask your mum and dad if they can supply 'dump' bins or boxes where you can store your bits and help give the impression of tidiness. Then agree a weekly date when you sort out and put away all your clothes so that your parents can see carpet. Stick to this.

They don't understand me!

It doesn't matter how well you get on with your parents, there will always be subjects and issues in life that are difficult, or impossible to discuss with them. This doesn't mean you're hopeless or that your mum and dad don't love or care about you, it's more to do with the fact that you're growing up and they may be finding that pretty difficult to come to terms with.

The things you
should be able
to talk to your
parents about,
but can't...

Sex or anything to do with it...

In an ideal world, as soon as you had any questions about the 'S' word, you'd simply sit down with your mum and dad and talk things through. If only it were that simple! Unfortunately, even bringing up the subject of sex with your parents can raise all sorts of issues, like...

No. 1 You're their baby and what on earth do you want to know about sex for? You're far too young to be thinking about that.

No. 2 Sit down and talk to your mum and dad about sex – yeah, right – that's not going to be at all embarrassing is it?

No. 3 If you do bring up the subject of sex, does that mean that every time your parents see you hanging around with a member of the opposite sex they're going to presume that the two of you are 'doing it'?

Talking to your parents about sex is never going to be easy for you or for them, but you may be surprised by their reaction if you do bring up the subject.

Give them a chance, and if it does all go horribly wrong, don't panic – there are plenty of people you can get advice and information from (see page 94-96).

'Now son, this is June, she is what we call "naked".'

Your body and the way it's changing...

Yet again, this is one of those 'issues' which only serves to remind your parents that you are growing up, which is why they may find it difficult to talk about it. However, they would probably hate the thought of you worrying yourself sick about what's going on 'down below' (or anywhere else for that matter), so don't let that put you off asking for their help or advice. If you're not sure you can handle talking to your parents about private parts, ask them if they could help you find a book or magazine article that tackles the subject. Or could they make an appointment for you to talk in private with a nurse at your local doctor's surgery about any worries you may have? Either way your parents will probably be relieved that you've turned to them for help, even if they don't directly give you the advice or info you're after.

Your taste in clothes, music, TV and the opposite sex...

Who knows what happens when parents become parents – but when they do, something certainly affects their taste in... well, everything really. It's almost not worth getting into discussions about what you like and why, because very, very rarely will they agree with you. So the next time your parents want to have that in-depth discussion about the state of 'pop' music, or 'the dreadful clothes young people are wearing these days', it's probably better to leave the room. Trust me, you don't want to go down that road.

'... and these are what we call T-R-A-I-N-E-R-S!'

Trouble at school with work, friends or bullying...

To your parents, school is the place where you go to learn the stuff that means you'll pass exams, which will lead to you getting a great job, which means you'll live happily ever after. Unfortunately, because it was some time ago that they were at school themselves, they've forgotten what a total nightmare the place can be. That's why you can get into difficulties when you try to talk to them about it. They forget that other than learning about compound fractions and split infinitives, school is also the place where you fall out with your friends, get bullied by older pupils and get picked on by certain teachers. Bear all this in mind if they don't seem to be taking your worries about school seriously, and don't suffer in silence – there are other people you can talk to (see page 94-96).

Can't communicate with your parents?

t's tough when the arguments and upsets at home really get you down, and one of the worst things about it is feeling so cut off and isolated in your own house. But don't think you're alone. You'd be surprised how many people just like you are going through similar problems...

Tell me about It

'I'm being bullied at school, but I really don't want my parents to get involved because they'll probably only make things worse.'
Sophie, 11

'Sometimes you start talking to your parents about a problem and just as you get going, you think, "Why did I ever bring this up?". Either they don't understand, but think they do, or once you've told them, they won't let it go, and then they'll go on and on about it. Especially if it's a problem with school!' **Liam, 13**

'My mum's OK about boys I suppose – she doesn't give me a hard time about them, but it's still embarrassing to talk to her about them. My dad on the other hand just makes fun of the whole situation which is really annoying.' **Amy, 13**

'The problem about talking to your mum about a school problem you may have is that she'll keep asking you if everything's OK and for ages afterwards will want to know what you're doing each day. Basically parents just get too interested, and you end up having to say, "Go away, leave me alone, I'll deal with it myself.".' **Stephen, 12**

'My parents don't seem to trust me any more. I keep explaining to them that I want more freedom but they just keep hassling me more and more. Their answer to everything these days seems to be, "You're only a teenage girl, you can't do that!".' **Kate, 13**

'I never talk to my mum about problems I'm having with my friends, because when I try she'll usually reply, "You're what with who? Who's Chantal?" I don't think she really knows that much about my life at all.' **Sonia, 14**

listen to me!

'Gosh, that sounds interesting dear!'

It's good to talk

'Calling dad, calling dad, mayday, mayday!'

When you're having trouble communicating with your parents it's worth bearing in mind that although you may have grown up thinking that they know the answers to everything – they don't! This doesn't mean you should shut down all lines of communication with them, or presume that they won't be interested or want to help if you've got a problem with something. It's always worth a try. But if things don't work out, don't get too frustrated or disappointed with them and try not to let it develop into an argument. There are alternatives...

all ears

Talking to... friends

Friends can often identify better with your problems because they may be going through similar things themselves. However, although they may be able to offer valuable support and advice, be aware that they won't know all the answers either. A good friend will admit that and help you find someone else who does.

Talking to... other members of the family

If you've tried talking to your mum or dad about something and you haven't got anywhere, it may be worth sounding out a brother or sister – especially if the problem you need to discuss is something to do with your home life, as they'll understand better than most. Another option is finding an adult who you trust and knows you well, but who isn't as involved as your parents – this is where aunts and uncles can come in handy. They'll have your best interests at heart and may have some great tips on handling your mum and dad – after all, they grew up with them.

'At least you understand me.'

Talking to... teachers

If the thought of sitting down for a cosy chat with your Geography teacher about your problems makes you want to laugh (or cry), just hold on a minute. Believe it or not, teachers are human, and when they're not busy trying to control a class of thirty distracted and uninterested teenagers they can be quite understanding and even helpful. If there really isn't one of your teachers who you feel comfortable talking to, ask around and see if any mates in other classes or years can suggest someone. It might be easier talking to a teacher you don't know anyway.

Talking to... organizations set up to help you

Whatever your problem is, and however lonely or isolated you might feel, there will always be someone out there to help. Although most people will have a laugh with their mates about the problem pages of teenage magazines, these can be a great source of advice and information.

After a few minutes reading these pages you'll soon realize that you're not the only person suffering with the problem you've got, you'll get sound advice from the Agony Aunt or Uncle, and if they can't help they'll give you the numbers and addresses of some brilliant organizations who can. Most of these organizations have free phone lines, and they won't ask for your name, address or telephone number.

Coping
with a family
Crisis

You've sussed out what it is that makes each member of your family tick, you've worked out how to negotiate your way out of an argument, and you've had a re-think on how to communicate with your parents. Blimey, it looks like you've got this family business cracked! But hang on a minute...

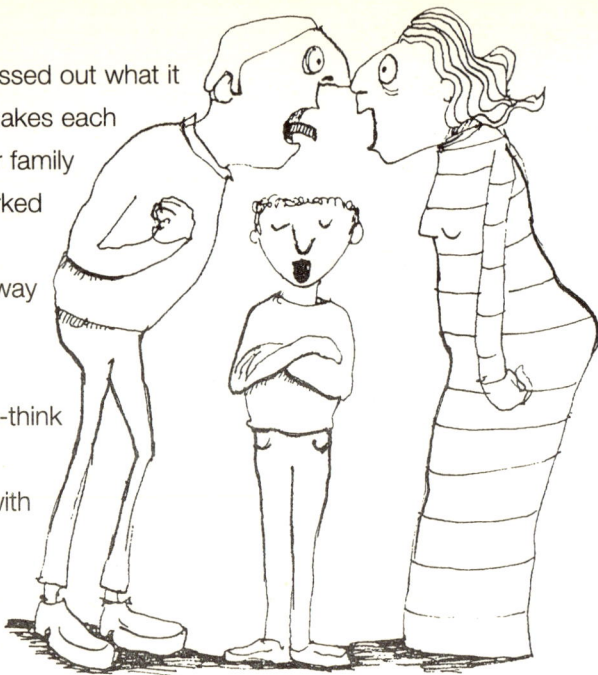

'Parents, I think it's time I got a pocket money rise.'

before you get too cocky and presume you've got it all sorted, be warned! Life has a nasty habit of springing things on you that you don't see coming.

Family break-up

Remember way back at the beginning of this book when the terrifying possibility of adults falling in love was mentioned? Well unfortunately they are just as capable of falling out of love with each other, even if these adults happen to be your mum and dad.

The 'D' word

If this happens in your house, you might not think it's very fair on you, and your parents certainly won't think it's much fun, but everyone in the family is going to need to deal with it. If your mum and dad aren't getting along and maybe they're thinking of separating or even getting a divorce, the first thing you'll realize is that life at home isn't going to be a bundle of laughs for a while. You may even feel that it's somehow your fault – if you hadn't kept going on about having more pocket money, or if you'd just shut up about staying out late – then maybe you wouldn't have stressed your parents out so much and this wouldn't have happened.

Speak up

For starters, don't blame yourself – parents are perfectly capable of messing things up all by themselves. Probably the best thing you can do in situations like this is give your mum and dad a bit of space to talk things through – and argue if necessary – but don't avoid speaking to them about what's going on. Let them know that you're aware there are problems, and that you'd rather they talked to you about it than pretend it isn't happening.

stay cool

facing facts

If your parents do eventually decide that it would be better for everyone concerned if they split up, you will probably have to choose which of them you will live with. Don't feel that you're being asked to choose which parent you love most, or who is 'your favourite' – they won't see it like that, as there are loads of other things that need to be taken into account when a decision like that is made, e.g. which parent is going to live nearest to your school and friends? Who will have the most space? What are each parent's work arrangements?

communication

Take the time to really think about what you want, and then when you're ready, talk to them about how you feel. If you can discuss things with both your mum and dad in a mature and reasoned way, they'll be better able to understand your point of view. This is a lot of responsibility for you to take on, and sometimes you may feel like you can't cope and you don't want to bother your mum and dad with your worries, but remember there are always other people you can talk to.

Tell me about it

'Mum and dad are always arguing at the moment. I think they're going to get divorced, but in a way that would be a relief if it stopped them rowing. I feel as if I'm caught in the middle. At night time when they're shouting at each other my sister will yell out to them to shut up and they'll talk quietly for a bit, but then they'll start up again. Sometimes I think it's best for them to get it out of their system.' **Kirsty, 11**

'When mum and dad split up it didn't seem like such a big deal because loads of my friends' parents are divorced.' **Dean, 12**

'In some ways I think it's better that mum and dad have split up and got on with their lives because it's made them both happier as individuals.' **Chris, 12**

'I do remember the day that mum and dad split up. I was six at the time. They used to argue quite a lot before it happened, and there always seemed to be an atmosphere in the house. Even after they split up the arguing continued but now they seem to get on OK. It was very hard at first because there would be times when I really wanted to see my dad and I couldn't. I really missed him.' **Eamon, 13**

be strong

Step Classes

Great! You've just about got used to the idea that your mum and
dad have split up and that family life has changed, so what do your
parents go and do? They meet someone else, fall in love and
decide to have another go at the happy family thing!

This may mean you inherit a new mum or dad, and even some new
brothers and sisters which, when you think about it, is a bit much!
After all your mum said 'No' to you when you wanted to bring a
gerbil home from school for the holidays, so why should you put up
with her moving in a whole flippin' new family!

Be Positive

However, sulking until
the cows come home
isn't going to make
this one go away.
Rather than presume
the worst about your
new found family, trust
your mum or dad's
instincts that their new
partner is 'an-alright-
sort-of-person', and
usually 'alright-sort-

of-people' tend to have 'OK-kind-of-kids'. Just because they're
'step-this' or 'step-that' shouldn't make the way you deal with them
any different to other members of the family... they'll just take a bit
of getting used to!

Tell me about it

'It was hard at first when my mum's new boyfriend moved in. I wanted her all to myself but I know that she wanted to meet someone really badly, so I was happy for her... but not for me.' **Laurie, 14**

'When I first inherited my step brother I thought he was alright, and my mum and her boyfriend didn't put any pressure on us to get on with each other. Now he can be a bit of a nightmare, but then I suppose most brothers are whether they're step ones or not.' **Tania, 14**

'I don't like talking to my dad about the problems I have with his girlfriend in case he takes her side. I'm also really worried because she's much younger than he is, and so she's still capable of having children, and I really don't want to have a half brother or sister.' **Sarah, 13**

'My step mum always seems to be very angry – sometimes she just can't seem to deal with me and I think part of the problem is that she doesn't like the thought of me having fun with my dad when she's not there. I don't worry too much about moaning about her to my dad though because he sometimes moans about her to me too!' **Ricky, 13**

'My step mum is the only one who treats me much younger than I am, but thankfully that doesn't influence my dad who's pretty relaxed about stuff.' **Fiona, 11**

oh no!

Scared to go home?

Home is supposed to be where you feel safest, and in an ideal world your family should be the people you turn to in times of trouble. Unfortunately this isn't the case for everybody, and in certain situations family members can be the cause of immense emotional distress or physical harm. There is a big difference between relatives 'getting on your nerves' and them mentally or physically abusing you, as these extracts from calls to ChildLine show.

'I'm scared of my big brother. He calls me names and picks on me all the time... he pushed me downstairs once, and is always beating up my sister too. Once he hurt her so badly, she had to go to hospital. He made me tell mum that it was an accident.' **Beth**

'Mum gets drunk every night – she has done for years. When she's drunk, she just starts shouting at us and dad starts shouting back... last night he got really angry and tried to strangle her. When I tried to stop him, he hit me... I don't want to live with them any more.' **Sarah**

'Dad found out that mum's been having an affair. They started arguing and he kicked her in the stomach. I just ran out of the house. Now I don't want to go back.' **Mandy**

'Ever since dad left, mum doesn't listen to me any more. She shouts at me and says, "I hate you, you're trouble". She's even threatened to throw me out of the house because I get on her nerves. She never says that to my little sister.' **Lucy**

It's difficult to imagine how anyone could cope in such terrible situations, and when you hear stories like these you realize how easy it must be for abuse victims to feel scared and alone. But despite the fact that they have been let down so badly by their family, there are other people and organizations out there who care and will help.

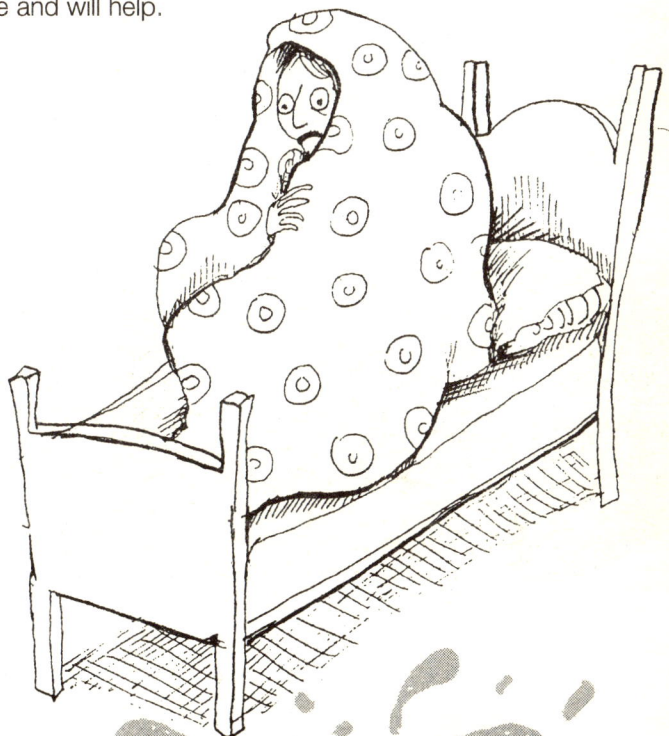

scared

Tell me about it

'My mum and dad split up, but now dad's come back to live with us. Everyone else in the family is really pleased but I don't want him to move back – I want them to get divorced. He's really mean to my mum. I used to see him tell her off, shout at her and then hit her. I don't believe he's changed.' **Susie**

'Dad's been horrible. He acts like he hates me, and it's been going on since last year when he lost his job, but lately it's been getting worse. He just shouts at me for no reason.' **Jayne**

'My mum has a new boyfriend and he's not nice to me, especially when mum's out. I can't tell her about it though, because she's been through a lot with my dad and she's really happy with Gary. I don't want to spoil it.' **Sam**

'Mum and dad are divorced and I live with mum. I visit dad sometimes, but last time I did he came into my room and showed me his private parts. I'm scared to go again in case it happens again.' **Natasha**

Don't suffer in silence

If you are the victim of any form of abuse, or know anyone else who is, it is incredibly important that you get help. Pretending that it isn't happening and keeping quiet about it isn't going to make it go away. Unfortunately abusive adults often rely on the fact that children are scared to tell anyone, which is why it is so important that you don't suffer in silence. Easier said than done, you may think, but there are people and organizations out there who will help. Every call to ChildLine, for example, is free and totally confidential – and they will be able to give you invaluable advice and information. Their 24–hour helpline number is 0800 1111.

Home Sweet Home? Make it happen!

However big or small a family problem may be, it's important that you do something about it rather than allowing it to take over your life and make you totally miserable. If the situation is as serious as the ones on pages 88 and 90 please seek help.

If, on the other hand your dilemma is more to do with the usual ups and downs of family life, think about the following...

Yes, they may drive you nuts at times.

No, they don't ever seem to understand you.

Yes, you may find yourself wondering how you got lumbered with the very odd people who live in your house.

But don't give up on your family totally just yet!

You might also want to ask yourself if there's just a teensy weensy possibility that, maybe, occasionally, the upheaval in your house might possibly have something to do with your behaviour?

Tell me about it

'I know it really winds my mum up when I don't answer her when she's asked me a question. I'll be watching the telly and she'll keep calling out my name, and I won't say anything until she comes into the room and has a go.'
Leo, 12

'I know that the amount of time I spend on the phone annoys my mum and dad. I make a lot of phone calls – I call at least one person every single night and I'll be on the phone for a minimum of 15 minutes and the calls can go on for three hours.' **Martin, 14**

'My mum's always having a go at me for being a slob. When I get home from school I just dump my bag down then go into the kitchen to get something to eat and half an hour later my bag and coat etc, will still be where I left them. It drives her mad.' **Denise, 12**

what, me?

'Dad, do you find that annoying?'

Come on, admit it... there are times when you're not always an innocent bystander in these minor family rows, so if you know that something you're doing or not doing is creating tension in your house and causing problems, it might be time to have a re-think. As a member of the family it's important to remember that you have responsibilities of your own, and if you show consideration, understanding and willingness to compromise in sticky situations, then you should get these things back in return when you really need them.

HELP!

If you want guidance dealing with a family problem, or if you need advice on other subjects that you feel your family can't help you with, don't panic! There are lots of organizations out there designed to offer free, confidential advice and information on a whole range of subjects...

Families
British Agencies for Adoption and Fostering 0171 593 2000
mail@baaf.org.uk
Gingerbread advice for lone parent families
Helpline: 0171 336 8184
National Family Mediation 0171 383 5993
general@nfn.org.uk
National Society for the Prevention of Cruelty to Children
(NSPCC) 24–hour child protection helpline: 0800 800 500
National Stepfamily Association and Parentline
(2–5pm, 7–10pm) 0990 168 388
Helpline: 01702 559 900 (9–9pm, Mon–Fri, 1–6pm, Sat)
Parents Anonymous gives help to parents who are tempted to abuse their children, and to those who have done so:
0171 263 8918

General
ChildLine Freepost 1111 London N1 OBR Helpline: 0800 1111
Children's Legal Centre 01206 873 820

Lifestyle and sexuality

Acceptance for parents of gay people: 01795 661 463

London Lesbian and Gay Switchboard 24–hour national helpline: 0171 837 7324

Bereavement

Child Death Helpline 0800 282 986 (Mon, Wed, Fri, 10–1pm; daily, 7–10pm)

Homelessness and runaways

Missing Persons Helpline 0500 700 700

Message Home Service freecall: 0800 700 740

Shelter 0171 505 2000

Emotional and mental health

The Acne Support Group 0181 561 6868

Depression Alliance 0171 633 9929

Eating Disorders Association 01603 619 090
eda@netcom.co.uk

Health Information Service they can refer you to a relevant organization for your problem and publish lots of useful information on a whole range of health issues: 0800 66 55 44

MIND (National Association for Mental Health) 0181 519 2122
info@mind.org.uk

Overeaters Anonymous 24–hour information line: 0700 784 985

Phobics Society 0161 881 1937

Samaritans 0345 90 90 90

Youth Access will refer you to a youth counselling service:
0181 772 9900

Young People's Information Centre
advice on a range of subjects: 01707 266 223

Alcohol and drugs

Alanon 24–hour helpline for families and friends of problem drinkers: 0171 403 0888

Drinkline Youth Dial-And-Listen 0800 91 78 282

National Drugs Helpline 0800 77 66 00

Contraception, pregnancy and sexual health

British Pregnancy Advisory
Service Action Line 0345 304 030

Brook Missed A Period Helpline 0171 617 0802

Brook Advisory Centres young people's info line:
0800 0185 023/ 0171 713 9000 (Mon–Fri, 9–5pm)

Contraceptive Education Service
England: 0171 837 4044 **Scotland:** 0141 576 5088
Wales: 01222 342 766 **N. Ireland:** 01232 325488

Family Planning Association 0171 837 4044

Ulster Pregnancy Advisory Service 01232 381 345

Violence and sexual abuse

Anti-Bullying Campaign 0171 378 1446
anti-bullying@compuserve.com

Kidscape they publish a free guide called *Beat Bullying*. For a copy, write enclosing two first class stamps, to 152 Buckingham Palace Rd, London SW1 9TR

NSPCC Child Protection 24–hour helpline: 0800 800 500

Rape and Sexual Abuse Support Line 01923 241 600

Refuge 24–hour domestic violence helpline: 0181 995 4430